MW01536773

The Inner Purpose of The Theosophical Society
And
Why i Became a Theosophist.
(2 Books)

Annie Besant

2017 by McAllister Editions (MCALLISTEREDITIONS@GMAIL.COM). This book is a classic, and a product of its time. It does not reflect the same views on race, gender, sexuality, ethnicity, and interpersonal relations as it would if it was written today.

CONTENTS

.

BOOK ONE

THE INNER PURPOSE OF THE THEOSOPHICAL SOCIETY

A speech delivered in 1898 at the Tenth Annual Convention of the European Section of the Theosophical Society.

IT falls to my lot to close this Tenth Annual Meeting of the European Section of the Society, and to close it by saying a few words on the inner purpose of the movement, on the future for which it is preparing, on the work which lies ready to its hand. You have heard from the President-Founder of the Society something of the road that lies now behind us something of the hopes that inspired those who on the physical plane gave the first impulse to the movement. You have heard from our brother from India something of the dangers of the road along which we are walking, something of the great ideal which inspires the hearts of all true Theosophists, as of all spiritually-minded men and women.

We may go a little further along these lines of thought that have been traced for us, and see how the inner purpose answers to the outer work, how the impulse from the spiritual plane came to incarnate itself in the world around us, how the true impulse came that made the Society, from Those who gave it and who give it its life, Those who sent it out on its blessed mission to the world, how They chose the time and the agents for accomplishing once more on earth the work so often begun and still unended - the work of sending the spiritual herald to announce a new step forward in the evolution of humanity, to mark out the pathway along which men should travel in accomplishing the stage thus opened, sounding the note which was to dominate the whole, stamping on it the mark which was to be the sign of the growing, making the principles known on which the form should be moulded, and giving to the world the life which was to find a new body on the material plane.

That inner purpose of-the Society may be said to be twofold: to the world at large, and to the members of the Society. To the world at large to herald the forward step to which I have just alluded; to the members of the Society to use them as the pioneers of that forward movement, making possible the road along which mankind should tread, hewing out, as it were, in front the path, smoothing that path with their own feet, giving their lives to make it possible - nay, even to make it comparatively easy - for those who should follow them. For as it is the glory of the Theosophical Society to herald the onward movement of the race, so it is the privilege of its early members to bear something of the burden which shall make that same burden lighter for the race that is to be born; to have the glory of the struggle though not of the victory; the glory of the sowing though not of the reaping; the scattering abroad of the seed of progress, leaving to others the glad days of harvest; content if in their day and generation they may make it possible that the great life beyond shall pour in fuller measure over the world so longing for its coming, and if they may be able by what they may learn - still more by what, having learned, they may practice - to raise in front of the race that is coming the ideal of a noble humanity, a humanity more divine than that which yet we have touched, making the ideal which the coming race shall partly realise, preparing the material out of which the statue of a divine humanity shall be hewn.

How shall that be done?

Glancing at the past, trying to learn the lessons of history that lie behind us, we see everywhere in history that when a new growth is coming to man, when a new stage of evolution is approaching and man stands on the threshold of a forward movement, that then from the great Elder Brothers of the race, from Those mighty Ones who are the spiritual Guardians of humanity, from Those who offer in Their own most sacred persons the perfect ideal of man become divine, where strength and tenderness, where wisdom and compassion are wedded in one perfect form and life - from Them, from Them alone, comes ever the impulse that guides humanity forward. And at every critical period of history, when a new race or family is to be born, there comes from Them alone the first impulse for the new advance, and also the outline of the form in which that advancing life is to be incarnate. Look back into the past and you will see that with the birth of each great family of our Aryan race a new religion has been given to the world, the religion before the people. You will find that the religion thus proclaimed by some Great One, taking birth among men as the Founder of the coming creed, you will find that in each case He gives His religion for the moulding of a new civilisation, for the shaping of a new type of humanity, for the building and the forming of a fresh body for the life, and that in the main points of the religion you can foretell the main outline of the dawning civilisation. That is true, as you will find if you care to study alike in the history of India where the first family of the Aryan race took root, or in the neighbouring country of Chaldea, where another shoot took its place and left its life and wisdom, or westward still, when you come to Greece and Rome of the Keltic race, with its great traditions of religion and philosophy - moulding the civilisation of beauty in Greece and the civilisation of law in Rome. You find the same with the later-born western nations, who received even ere they lay in their cradle the great teaching of the Christ, to be to them what the teachings of His predecessors were to the nations to whom they were given, and to shape the western civilisation as the Others had shaped the civilisations that went before. And when we find in history that the coming of a new spiritual impulse has ever meant a forward step for man, when we find that the nature of that impulse has outlined the nature of the coming evolution - then what must we think when we see come another mighty impulse from the same immortal source, and what can we learn as we scan the characteristics of that impulse, as to the nature of the growth which lies next in space and time before the advancing feet of man?

One great difference comes at once - springing as it were before our eyes - when we look at the difference between this movement and the others that have gone before it - a difference so great, so vital, so fundamental, that if we can see its meaning, some of the steps at least become clear before us; that if we can assimilate its significance, we have a veritable touchstone whereby we may test everything around us in science, in philosophy, and in politics, an Ithuriel spear as it were which we can use to touch every form that comes before us, to see whether within the form is hidden an angel of light, or whether there is veiled within some dangerous misleading demon who would draw humanity astray from the path which it ought to tread.

What is that mark, that unique characteristic?

Every great Teacher coming to the world has brought as His priceless gift to man some new proclamation of spiritual truth in the form of a new religion. This movement alone, of all the great religious impulses of the past, brings no new religion to mankind, proclaims in no new formal shape the world-message, calls no men to come apart from other faiths and other creeds and place themselves within a pale, which, while it shuts them in for special teaching, shuts others out as not members of the faith, as outside its special proclamation. Alone of all the impulses it speaks, not of a new religion, but of the common basis of all religions alike. Differing from all that went before, it does not build a new church, it does not found a new philosophy, it does not raise a wall of separation round those who accept it, those who reject it being without. It proclaims one basis for all. It teaches religion, and not a religion; that which is common to all, not that which shall be special to a new church or a new faith. It makes its basis in the unity of all its forerunners, so that it joins all together instead of adding a new one to the many faiths of the world. That is its great mark, that its unique characteristic- one belief for all in one spiritual life, one common evolution, one goal which all may approach, and approach by different roads. Every road right for those who walk in it; every road divine, and men able to reach God therein.

So at the beginning of our race was it stated, and now practically that is put before the world as the stage that it should try to realise; every man remaining in his own road, every man remaining in his own religion, no converting from one faith equally divine to another, no proselytising in one faith by another; all faiths equally divine, for all have one source and seek one goal; every man of every race right in his own religion and only wrong when he denies the inspiration of the religion of his brothers; right whenever he raises loving hands in worship, wrong whenever he pushes out angry hands in rejection; right whenever in his worship he knows that all languages are one in the ears of the Divine that hears them, wrong only when he thinks his voice the only one that can pierce the heavens and reach the divine throne; wrong when he denies to his brothers the same Fatherhood that he claims as his own.

The unity of every faith that loves God and serves man, that is the message which comes to the world as the inner purpose of the Theosophical movement: to draw all faiths together, to see them all as sisters, not as rivals, to join all religions in one golden chain of divine love and human service. That is the purpose of our movement all the world over - to reverence and serve religion wherever we find it, and to pierce through the varieties of the outer faith to the unity of the hidden life.

That, then, our work. But if that be our work, then are we not false to it in its most essential meaning, if anywhere we carry strife instead of peace and speak words of exclusion instead of words of love? They only are the true Theosophists, they only reflect in small degree the spirit of the great

Brotherhood of Teachers, they only are worthy messengers, however feeble, of their divine message who carry out the spirit of brotherhood amid all the warring creeds, and who not only carry the message of peace, but live the peace they teach,, and show the ideal of brotherhood in life as thoroughly as they proclaim its reality in words.

But what does it foretell for the future? It foretells the dawning of a civilisation where unity shall be the keynote instead of strife; where co-operation shall be the means of life rather than competition; where beyond the development of the individual in the combative intellect, the spiritual unity shall begin to dawn in the eyes and in the lives of men. For as surely as this truth is given in spiritual form, as surely as the existence of that spiritual brotherhood of man is a fundamental truth in nature, so also it is true that the life must find its fit form in which to incarnate, and that deeper understanding, closer bonds, more real love between nations now apart, shall tread in the wake of the Theosophical movement, and shall bring in due course of time to the earth we live in a peace which at present lives only in the higher regions of the universe. That is the promise which it lifts before our eyes, despite the struggle of the warring world; that the hope - full of peace and bliss - which it points to in the future beyond the battle-field and the massacre, beyond the poverty and the misery, beyond the heart-break of the present, into the heart-joy of the future. The work to which we are called is to form a nucleus of souls at one, to show by our lives the unity we proclaim, to live love in a world of hatred, to live peace in a world of strife. That, and nothing less than that, the high mission to which we are called; that, and nothing less than that, the noble duty that is bound upon our shoulders; and just in proportion as we live it, we shall make it possible for others; just in proportion as our lives are its preachers, will the sermon take effect on the hearts of men.

But if you realise that, what can shake you in your devotion to this movement? What can trouble your serene confidence in the certainty of the joy that lies beyond? The Society in its outer form may be shaken over and over again. It is well that it should be shaken from time to time, for how can the weak and the strong be separated - as they must be separated for a while until the hardest of the battle is over -save by so shaking the Society that only those whose vision is clear, whose hearts are brave, whose wills are strong, shall be able to stay within the pioneer band who are hewing out the road to the future? The place of the weak is not in the forefront of the struggle. The place of the weak is not in the worst shock of the combat. Rather, easier strife for them, an easier pathway, sufficiently difficult to draw out their strength, but not difficult enough to drive them to despair. For those who are strong, as we heard just now, for them the place of hardest fight and keenest struggle, and those who would be the pioneers of the future must be willing to bear and strong to endure. Theirs the place within the forward rank of the movement, making possible for the weaker the treading of the up-hill path.

Matters it then to us, if this be true, that our thought shall spread everywhere without our name? Rightly did our President tell us that all over the world these thoughts were moving, and that within the limits of the different faiths you find the Theosophical ideas proclaimed. That is the testimony to the reality of our work, that the only reward that it is well that we should look for - not that we shall be known as leaders, but that the ideas may permeate throughout the civilisation in which we are living; not that our names shall stand high as teachers, not that our names shall be known as thinkers, but that the teaching shall spread everywhere, no matter what lips proclaim it; that the knowledge shall spring up on every side, no matter by whom that knowledge at any time be given. Enough to sow; let anyone have the name of the sowing to whom it may happen to come;

let those who can only work when they are praised, let them have the credit of spreading the ideas everywhere. Let us be content with the noble work of labouring, so that the ideas may go everywhere, and let every church take them as its own - they *are* its own if it only knew the treasures that its Teacher gave it. Ours enough to point out where they may be found, and let others hold them up before the eyes of the world. Those who are able to reach the people, let them take the truth and speak it, so that everywhere its sound may be heard. When from Christian pulpit a Theosophical truth is taught, let all our hearts see in that the reward for which we have been labouring. If our Master's truth be told, what matters it who shall tell it? If any eyes see His beauty, what matters whose hand it is that lets fall the veil?

For those of you who are members of this great Society, who hold it the highest privilege that Karma could bring to you to be one of the workers in this movement for humanity, for you what is the future offered you, for you what the prize of the high calling which is in the far future to-day? To know what Those who have gone before us have known, so that our knowledge may be used for the helping of the ignorance of the world; to tread the path which Those have trodden before us, that narrow, ancient path that is opened for us by the Sages and can only be shut to us by our own weakness, by our own folly, by our own sin. No other hand in heaven or earth can close the gateway of that path against any human soul; only its own hand can close it, for thus hath spoken the law. To you the path is clear in sight, proclaimed again in the hearing of all. Coming into the Society you take, as it were, your first step in that direction of which the ending is to be one of the Saviours of the world.

What magic lies in those four words! What music in the inspiration which they bring to the human soul! To be a world-Saviour - what does it mean? It means that all the world's ignorance is less because you know; that all the world's sin is lass because you are pure; that all the world's sorrow is less because you are sharing it; that all the world's weakness is less because you lend to it your strength. Struggle to be strong, not in order that you may be strong, but that world may be stronger. Struggle to be wise, not that you may be wise, but that the world may be the wiser. Struggle to be pure, not that you may be pure, but that the whole world may be nearer to the purity that is divine. Care not for your own joy, for your own happiness, for your own satisfaction. Care only for the upward treading of the world and the little help you may bring to it. You must either be lifted or lift. You must either be a clog or wings to lift the world upward on its road. That is the great choice which lies before you in coming into this movement.

Your Self has chosen that destiny even if your brain as yet knows it not. That your brain may know it us your Self knows it, that your intellect may recognise it as your Self has recognised it - that may be the outcome of your worship, of your devotion, of your learning; for this only is worth living for - that the world maybe better because we have been living in it; this only is the one crown of humanity - that the man crowns himself with thorns in order that others may be crowned with life immortal.

THE THIRD OBJECT OF THE THEOSOPHICAL SOCIETY

A MEMBER asked me a few days ago: *Have we not as a Society rather neglected our Third Object? Very few have investigated the powers latent in man at first-hand. Is not the time coming when the Third Object should receive more attention?*

We, who are members of the Society, have we attended to it? Perhaps not very assiduously. There are obviously two ways of investigating. People may make experiments for themselves, or they may study the experiments made by others. The latter method is that which is usually employed in the study of most sciences. It is only a few of us who take up any science and actually experimentalize in it. All of us at school long ago learnt something of astronomy; but I hardly imagine that many of you bought a large telescope and went into the study at first-hand. It happens that I did; therefore I may say that I have a little first-hand knowledge of astronomy. Naturally, most of my information on the subject comes from books; I cannot pretend to have made astronomical investigations in the sense of trying to discover anything new; but I have at least confirmed something of what I have read in the books; and most people do not even go so far as that. I suppose that it is the same with many sciences. A person may know a great deal about any subject without having actually tackled it himself.

So you will be doing something in order to learn about the powers latent in man if you read carefully what has been written of them, if you try to understand what these powers are, and to convince yourself of their reality by studying the enormous mass of printed evidence. Of course, you can do a good deal more if you take the thing in hand and try for yourself. A number of our members have been encouraged to do this, and a great deal of instruction has been given in regard to meditation, which is one of the safest of the methods of approaching this subject experimentally. But not all methods are safe; we have to remember that investigation at first-hand into the development of psychic powers has its dangers, and the tradition of our Society has always been to discourage people from rash experiments - I think quite rightly.

Many books have been written upon Yoga practices - some of them, I fear, by people who have little practical acquaintance with the subject; and in a number of cases harm has resulted from ill-judged attempts to follow the directions given. I am told that there are Indian Yogis who give instruction in these arts; but the Yogi usually teaches only those who are definitely his pupils and follow him everywhere. He therefore has his experimenters always under observation, and can at once check anyone who may be running into danger; whereas the man who learns his Yoga from a book has no such safeguard. I have myself received a large number of applications for help from persons who have seriously injured their brains, their nervous system, and their constitution generally, by plunging blindfold into this kind of psychism; and, sadly, often no effective help can be given. It is so easy to lose one's balance - so terribly difficult to regain it. That is why our beloved President has forbidden the sale of such books at any of the Theosophical shops under her direction.

The President at least has been most careful not to give any dangerous advice, and has explained to her pupils that they should at once stop all meditation if any dangerous symptoms appear - even such as a headache. Those to whom psychic unfoldment comes fairly naturally, who would therefore be in very little danger, have been able to make progress along this line. But no one wants to be responsible for people risking their lives or their reason, and consequently those who know something about the subject have been exceedingly careful as to what they said. I personally made no attempt in that direction at all, until it was suggested to me by my Master that I might with advantage make certain experiments. I took that to mean that he would watch over them, so I made the experiments and the endeavour succeeded; but I dare not advise any other person to do the same thing. I suppose the Master satisfied himself that in my case it could be done safely. I must not describe the method - indeed, I promised not to do so; but I have written what little I may as to the later stages of the training in my booklet *How Theosophy Came to Me.*

Still, there are certain things that we can all try without danger. The scheme of meditation which I have suggested in the final chapter of several of my books is quite harmless; but remember that you must not overstrain. These operations do involve a certain strain, whatever line is adapted; but they should not involve direct pain of any sort. In ail such cases, we are working either with the higher vehicles altogether, or if we are using chiefly the physical brain, we are trying to make it do a little more than it is intended to do; and that is always a dangerous thing to attempt, so it must be done with the greatest care, and very gradually.

"Have we neglected our Third Object?" We have always been told that the development of psychic faculty is not a necessity till a certain rather advanced stage is reached. Obviously, then, what we have to do first of all is to work at our character. Most of us find that there is still something to do along that line. My own plan, as I have already said, was to wait until I was directly told by my Master to move. That is absolutely safe, of course. Many of us might be willing to run a small risk for the sake of making some definite attempt in that direction; but that is, naturally, a man's own responsibility.

It is an uncertain undertaking, for no one can tell when any result will be reached. Some people with slight effort obtain at least indications that psychic powers may open; others try for a long time without any observable effect. At any time the man steadily working may break through, and no one ever knows how near he may be to success. On the other hand, we are bound to tell enquirers that we do not know how long or how difficult it will be. No person undertaking to train another could *promise* anything; even if he could see the past karma of the applicant, it would still be impossible to speak with certainty.

The intermediate stage of carefully studying the subject is always open to us, and is always useful. Study the case of the people in whom such powers are developed. I myself learnt a good deal about such things before I made any attempt to advance in them myself. I went into the Highlands of Scotland to examine cases of what is called " second-sight". That is a bad name for it - it is really foresight. I examined very many cases, and absolutely satisfied myself that this strange foresight is possible, though without trying any experiments of my own. I think such a course might be called study of the powers latent in man, and of course it is open to anyone.

Then there are experiments in telepathy or psychometry; many people can do something in that way with a little practice. Then there is always spiritualism, although the latter is chiefly concerned with trying to prove the return of the dead to earth. A great deal in mediumship, however, indicates the possession of latent powers by man; though spiritualists preach the idea from another side, and wish a man to be absolutely passive and lay himself open to influences of all sorts, which we consider unsafe.

The line recommended to us has always been to try to develop your own powers; to be active, not passive. It is true that the spiritualist tries first of all to engage a "spirit-guide" - some dead person who will act as a sort of guardian to the medium, and drive away all evil influences, while leaving him open to what is good. But this is not always sufficient; I have seen one case, at least, in which a spirit-guide was absolutely overpowered by an evil entity; and if a certain great person had not been physically present at that séance, it would have meant death for one or two people. So the spiritualistic method of investigation is not to be unreservedly recommended.

THE END.

BOOK TWO

WHY I BECAME A THEOSOPHIST.

Endurance is the crowning qualify

And patience all the passion of great hearts;

These are their stay, and when the leaden world

Sets its hard face against their fateful thought

And brute strength, like a scornful conqueror.

Clangs his huge mace down in the other scale,

The inspired soul but flings its patience in.

And slowly that outweighs the ponderous globe.

One faith against a whole world's unbelief,

One soul against the flesh of all mankind.—Lowell.

GROWTH necessarily implies change, and, provided the change be sequential and of the nature of development, it is but the sign of intellectual life. No one blames the child because it has outgrown its baby-clothes, nor the man when his lad's raiment becomes too narrow for him; but if the mind grows as well as the body, and the intellectual garment of one decade is outgrown in the following, cries are raised of rebuke and of reproach by those who regard fossilization as a proof of mental strength. Just now from some members of the Freethought party reproaches are being levelled at me because I have avowed myself a Theosophist. Yet of all people Freethinkers ought to be the very last to protest against change of opinion per se for almost every one of them is a Freethinker by virtue of mental change, and the only hope of success for their propaganda in a Christian country is that they may persuade others to pass through a similar change. They are continually reproaching Christians in that their minds are not open to argument, will not listen to reason; and yet if one of themselves sees a further truth and admits it, they object as much to the open mind of the Freethinker as to the closed mind of the Christian.

To take up the position assumed by some of my critics is to set up a new infallibility, as indefensible, and less venerable, than that of Rome. It is to claim that the summit of human knowledge has been reached by them, and that all new knowledge is folly. It is to do what Churches in all ages have done, to set up their own petty fences round the field of truth, and in so doing to trace the limits of their own cemeteries. And for the Freethinker to do this is to be false to his creed, and to stain himself with the most flagrant inconsistency; he denounces the immovability of the Church as obstinacy, while he glorifies the immovability of the Freethinker as strength; he blames the one because it shuts its ears against his new truth, and then promptly shuts his own ears against new truth from some one else.

Let us distinguish; there is a vacillation of opinion which is a sign of mental weakness, a change which is a turning back.

When all the available evidence for a doctrine has been examined, and the doctrine thereupon has been rejected, it shows a mental fault somewhere if that doctrine be again accepted, the evidence remaining the same. It does not, on the other hand, imply any mental weakness, if, on the bringing forward of new evidence which supplies the lacking demonstration, the doctrine previously rejected for lack of such evidence be accepted. Nor does it imply mental weakness if a doctrine, accepted on certain given evidence, be later given up on additions being made to, knowledge.

Only in this way is intellectual progress made; only thus, step by step, do we approach the far-off Truth. A Freethinker, who has become one by study and has painfully wrought out his freedom, discarding the various doctrines of

Christianity, could not rebelieve them without confessing either that he had been hasty in his rejection or was insecure in his adhesion; in either case he would have shown intellectual weakness. But not to the Freethinker can be closed any new fields of mental discovery; not on his limbs shall be welded the fresh fetters of a new orthodoxy, after he has hewn off the links of the elder faith; not round his eyes, facing the sunshine, shall be bound the bandage of a cramping creed; not to him shall Atheism, any more than Theism, say: "Thus far shalt thou think, and no further." Atheism has been his deliverer; it must never be his gaoler: it has freed him; it must never tie him down.

Grateful for all it has saved him from, for all it has taught him, for the strength it has given, the energy it has inspired, the eager spirit of man yet rushes onward, crying: " The light is beyond!" I maintain, then, that the Freethinker is bound ever to keep open a window towards new light, and to refuse to pull down his mental blinds. Freethought, in fact, is an intellectual state, not a creed; a mental attitude, not a series of dogmas. No one turns his back on Freethought who subjects every new doc trine to the light of reason, who weighs its claims without prejudice, and accepts or rejects it out of loyalty to truth alone. It seems necessary to recall this fundamental truth about Freethought, in protest against the position taken up by some of my critics, who would fain identify a universal principle with a special phase of nineteenth century Materialism. The temple of Freethought is not identical with the particular niche in which they stand.

Nor is the Freethought platform so narrow a stage as Mr. Foote would make out in his recent attack on me. He accuses me of using the Freethought platform "in an unjustifiable manner," because I have lectured on Socialism from it, and he is afraid that I may lecture on Theosophy from it and "lead Freethinkers astray." I have hitherto regarded Freethinkers as persons competent to form their own judgment, not mere sheep to be led one way or the other. There is a curious clerical ring in the phrase, as though free ventilation of all opinions were not the very life-blood of Freethought. It is a new thing to seek to exclude from the Freethought platform any subject which concerns human progress. In his younger and broader days Mr. Foote lectured from the Freethought platform on Monarchy, Republicanism, the Land Question, and Literature, and no one rebuked him for unjustifiable use of it; now he apparently desires to restrict it to attacks on Theology alone. I protest against this new-fangled narrowing of the grand old platform, from which Carlile, Watson, Hetherington, and many another fought for the right of Free Speech on every subject that concerned human welfare, a noble tradition carried on in our own time by Charles Bradlaugh, who has always used the Freethought platform for political and social, as well as anti-theological, work. I know that of late years Mr. Foote has narrowed his own advocacy, but that gives him no claim to enforce on others a similar narrowness, and to denounce their actions as unjustifiable when they carry on the use of the platform which has always been customary. For my own part, I have so used it since I joined the Freethought party. I have lectured on Radicalism and on Socialism, on Science and on Literature, as well as on Theology, and I shall continue to do so.

Of course if the National Secular Society should surrender its motto, "We seek for truth," and declare, like any other sect, that it has the whole truth, there are many who would have to reconsider their position as members of it. If the National Secular Society should follow Mr. Foote's recent departure, and seek to exclude from its platform all non-theological subjects, it has the right to do so, though it ought then to drop the name of Secular and call itself merely the Anti-Theological Society; but until it does, I shall follow the course I have followed these fifteen years, of using the platform for lecturing on any subject that seems to me to be useful.

When the National Secular Society excludes me from its platform I must of course submit, but no one person has a right to dictate to the Society what matters it shall discuss. A few weeks ago a Branch of the National Secular Society wrote asking me to lecture on Theosophy: was I to answer that the subject was not a suitable one for them to consider? Mr. Foote in one breath blames me for not explaining my position to the Freethought party, and in the next warns me off the platform from which the explanation can best be made. I had no paper in which I could give my reasons for becoming a Theosophist, and I am told that to use the platform is unjustifiable! Leaving this, I pass to the special subject of this paper, "Why I became a Theosophist." Mr. Foote writes, with exceeding bitterness, that, "amidst all her changes Mrs. Besant remains quite positive."

What are all these changes? Like Mr. Foote and most of the rest of us, I passed from Christianity into Atheism. After fifteen years, I have passed into Pantheism. The first change I need not here defend; but I desire to say that in all I have written and said, as Atheist, against super naturalism, I have nothing to regret, nothing to unsay. On the negative side Atheism seems to me to be unanswerable; its case against supernaturalism is complete. And for some years I found this enough: I was satisfied, and I have remained satisfied, that the universe is not explicable on supernatural lines. But I turned then to scientific work, and for ten years of patient and steadfast study I sought along the lines of Materialistic Science for answer to the questions on Life and Mind to which Atheism, as such, gave no answer. During those ten years I learned, both at second hand from books and at first hand from nature, something of what was known of living organisms, of their evolution and their functions. Building on a sound knowledge of Biology I went on to Psychology, still striving to follow nature into her recesses and to wring some answer from the Eternal Sphinx. Everywhere I found collecting of facts, systematizing of knowledge, tracing of sequences; nowhere one gleam of light on the question of questions:

"What is Life? What is Thought?"

Not only was Materialism unable to answer the question, but it declared pretty positively that no answer could ever be given. While claiming its own methods as the only sound ones, it declared that those methods could not solve the mystery. As Professor Lionel Beale says (quoted in "Secret Doctrine," vol. i, p. 540): "There is a mystery in life—a mystery which has never been fathomed, and which appears greater, the more deeply the phasnomena of life are studied and contemplated. In living centers—far more central than the centers seen by the highest magnifying powers, in centers of living matter, where the eye cannot penetrate, but towards which the understanding may tend—proceed changes of the nature of which the most advanced physicists and chemists fail to afford us the conception: nor is there the slightest reason to think that the nature of these changes will ever be ascertained by physical investigation, inasmuch as they are certainly of an order or nature totally distinct from that to which any other phenomenon known to us can be relegated." Elsewhere he remarks: "Between the living state of matter and its nonliving state there is an absolute and irreconcilable difference; that, so far from our being able to demonstrate that the nonliving passes by gradations into, or gradually assumes the state of condition of, the living, the transition is sudden and abrupt; and that matter already in the living state may pass into the non-living condition in the same sudden and complete manner.

... The formation of bioplasm direct from non-living matter is impossible even in thought, except to one who sets absolutely at nought the facts of physics and chemistry." ("Bioplasm," pp. 3 and 13.) Under these circumstances, it was no longer a matter of suspending judgment until knowledge made the judgment possible, but the positive assurance that no knowledge could be obtained on the problem posited. The instrument was confessedly unsuitable, and it became a question of resigning all search into the essence of things, or finding some new road. It may be said: "Why seek to solve the insoluble?" But such phrase begs the question. Is it insoluble because one method will not solve it? Is light incomprehensible because instruments suitable for acoustics do not reveal its nature? If from the blind clash of atoms and the hurtling of forces there comes no explanation of Life and Mind, if these remain sui generis, if they loom larger and larger as causes rather than as effects, who shall blame the searcher after Truth when, failing to find how Life can spring from force and matter, he seeks whether Life be not itself the Center, and whether every form of matter may not be the garment wherewith veils itself an Eternal and Universal Life?

RIDDLES IN PSYCHOLOGY.

No one, least of all those who have tried to understand some thing of the "riddle of this painful universe," will pretend that Materialism gives any answer to the question, "How do we think?" or throws any light on the nature of thought. It traces a correlation between living nervous matter and intellection; it demonstrates a parallelism between the growing complexity of the nervous system and growing complexity of phenomena of consciousness; it proves that intellectual manifestations may be interfered with, stimulated, checked, altogether stopped, by acting upon cerebral matter; it shows that certain cerebral activities, normally accompany psychical activities. That is, it proves that on our globe, necessarily the only place in which its investigations have been carried on, there is a close connection between living nervous matter and thought-processes.

As to the nature of that connection knowledge is dumb, and even theory can suggest no hypothesis. Materialism regards thought as a function of the brain; "the brain secretes thought," says Carl Vogt, "as the liver secretes bile." It is a neat phrase, but what does it mean? In every other bodily activity organ and function are on the same plane. The liver has form, color, resistance, it is an object to the senses; its secretion approves itself to those same senses, as part of the Object World;-the cells of the liver come in contact with the blood, take from it some substances, reject others, recombine those they have selected, pour them out as bile. It is all very wonderful, very beautiful; but the sequence is unbroken; matter is acted upon, analysed, synthesised afresh; it can be subjected at every step to mechanical processes, inspected, weighed; it is matter at the beginning, matter all through, matter at the end; we never leave the objective plane. But "the brain secretes thought?" We study the nerve-cells of the brain; we find molecular vibration; we are still in the Object World, amid form, color, resist adce, motion. Suddenly there is a Thought, and all is changed.

We have passed into a new world, the Subject World; the thought is formless, colorless, intangible, imponderable; it is neither moving nor motionless; it occupies no space, it has no limits; no processes of the Object World can touch it, no instrument can inspect. It can be analysed, but only by Thought: it can be measured, weighed, tested, but only by its own peers in its own world. Between the Motion and the Thought, between the Object and the Subject, lies an unspanned gulf, and Vogt's words but darken counsel; they are misleading, a false analogy, pretending likeness where likeness there is none.

Many perhaps, as I have said, like myself, beginning with somewhat vague and loose ideas of physical processes, and then, on passing into careful study, dazzled by the radiance of physiological discoveries, have hoped to find the causal nexus, or have, at least, hoped that hereafter it might be found by following a road rendered glorious by so much new light. But I am bound to say, after the years of close and strenuous study both of physiology and psychology to which I have alluded, that the more I have learned of each the more thoroughly do I realize the impassability of the gulf between material motion and mental process, that Body and Mind, however closely intermingled, are twain, not one.

Let us look a little further into the functions of Mind, as e. g., Memory. How does the Materialist explain the phenomena of Memory? A cell, or group of cells, has been set vibrating; hence a thought. Similar vibrations are continually being set up, and every cell in the cerebrum must have been set vibrating millions of times during infancy, youth, and maturity. The man of fifty remembers a scene of his childhood; that is, a group of cells—every atom of which has been changed several times since the scene occurred—sets up a certain series of vibrations which reproduces the original series, or let us say the chief of the original series, and so gives rise to the remembrance, the vibration being prior in time, necessarily, to the remembrance. I will not press the further difficulty as to the initiation of this motion and the complexities of the "Association" in intensifying vibration so as to bring the thought above the threshold of consciousness.

It will suffice to try and realize what is implied in the setting up of this series of vibrations, each cell vibrating in conjunction with its fellows as it vibrated forty years before, despite the myriad other combinations possible, each one of which would cause other thought. A well-stored memory contains thousands of "thought pictures;" each of these must have its vibratory cell-series in the human cerebrum. Is this possible, having regard to the laws of space and time, to which, be it remembered, cell-vibrations are subject? But these difficulties are on the surface; let us go a step further. In dealing with psychology, we must study the abnormal as well as the normal. Normally, thought results from senseimpression; abnormally, sense-impression may result from thought.

Thus, a young officer was told off to exhume the corpse of a person some time buried; as the coffin came into view the effluvium was so overpowering that he fainted. Opened, the coffin was found to be empty. It was the vivid imagination of the young man that had created the sense-impression, for which there was no objective cause. Again, a novelist, absorbed in his plot, in which one of his characters was killed by arsenic, showed symptoms of arsenical poisoning. Here the oesophagus, and stomach were affected by a cause that existed only in the mind. I have failed to find any Materialist explanation of a large group of phenomena, of which these are types.

Take again the extraordinary keenness of perception found in some cases of disease. A patient suffering from one of certain disorders will hear words spoken at a distance far beyond that of ordinary audition. It seems as though the lowering of muscular power and of general vitality coincided with the intensifying of the perceptive faculties—a fact difficult to explain from the Materialist standpoint, though the explanation saute aux yeux from the Theosophical, as will be seen further on.

Or consider the phenomena of clairvoyance, clairaudience, and thought-transference. Here, if a person be thrown into an abnormal nerve condition, he can see and hear at distances which preclude normal vision and audition. A clairvoyant will read with eyes bandaged, or with a board interposed between reader and book. He will follow the closed or opened hand of the mesmeriser, and give its position and condition. Here, I do not give special instances, as the cases are legion and are easily accessible to anyone who desires to investigate. A large number of careful experiments have put cases of thought-transference beyond possibility-of reasonable denial, and can be referred to by the student. I cannot burden this short pamphlet with them, especially as it is merely intended as a tracing of the road along which I have travelled, not as an exposition of the whole case against Materialism.

Mesmerism and hypnotism, again, suggest the existence in man of faculties which are normally latent. All sense-perception in the mesmerised is overcome by the will of the mesmeriser, who imposes on him "sense-perceptions" antagonistic to facts: e. g., he will drink water with enjoyment as wine, with repugnance as vinegar, etc. The body is mastered by the mind of another, and responds as the operator wills. Experiments in hypnotism have yielded the most astounding results; actions commanded by the hypnotiser being performed by the person hypnotised, although the two were separated by distance, and some time had elapsed since the hypnotic operation had been performed, and the person hypnotised restored apparently to the normal conditions. (See the experiments of Dr. Charcot and others.) So serious have been the results of these experiments that a society is now in course of formation in London, which seeks to restrict the practice of hypnotism to the medical profession and persons duly and legally qualified to practice it.

"For this purpose," says the acting Secretary, "it is proposed to found a school of hypnotism in London, at which the science will be properly taught by the best exponents, scientifically demonstrated by lecture and experiment, and its beneficial uses correctly defined and expounded." Dr. Charcot has used hypnotism in the place of anaesthetics, and has successfully performed a dangerous operation on a hypnotised patient, whose heart was too weak to permit the use of chloroform. Dr. Grillot uses it for "moral cures," and hypnotises dishonest persons into honesty. The Rev. Arthur Tooth is using it successfully for the cure of dipsomaniacs and relief of pain.

Allied to these are the phenomena of double-consciousness, many records of which are preserved in medical works; here, in some cases, a double life has been led, no memory of one state existing in the other, and each life on reentering a state being taken up where it was dropped on leaving it.. With only one brain to function, how can this duality of consciousness be explained? Hallucinations, visions of all kinds, again, do not seem to me reducible under any purely Materialist hypothesis: "matter and motion" do not solve these phenomena of the psychic world.

Another riddle in psychology is that of dreams. If thought be the result only of molecular vibration, how can dreams occur in which many successive events and prolonged arguments occupy but a moment of time? Vibrations, I again remind the reader, are subject to the conditions of space and time. Succession of thoughts must imply succession of vibrations on the Materialist hypothesis, and vibrations take time; yet thousands of these, which, waking, would occupy days and weeks, are compressed into a second in a dream.

Quite another class of phenomena is that in which abilities are manifested for which no sufficient cause can be discovered.

Infant prodigies, like Hofmann and others, whence come they? We know what the brain of a very young child is like, and we find young Hofmann improvising with a scientific knowledge that he has not had time to acquire in the ordinary way. "Genius," we say, with our fashion of pretending to explain by using a word; but how can Materialism, which will have matter give birth to thought, find in the newly-made brain of this child the cerebral modifications necessary for producing his melodies? And when a servant in a farmhouse, ignorant in her waking hours, talks Hebrew in her sleep, how are we to regard her brain from a Materialist standpoint? Or when the calculating boy answers a complex calculation when the words are scarcely out of the questioner's mouth, how have the cells performed their duties? a problem that becomes the more puzzling when we find that the increase of circulation, etc., which normally accompany brain activity, have not, in his case, occurred.

These are only a few riddles out of many, but they are samples of the bulk. To some of us they are of overpowering interest, because they seem to suggest dimly new fields of thought, new possibilities of development, new heights which Humanity shall hereafter scale. We do not believe that the forces of Evolution are exhausted. We do not believe that the chapter of Progress is closed. When a new sense was developing in the past its reports at first must have been very blundering, often very misleading, doubtless very ridiculous at times, but none the less had it the promise of the future, and was the germ of a higher capacity. May not some new sense be developing today, of which the many abnormal manifestations around us are the outcome? Who, with the past behind him, shall dare to say, "It cannot be?" and who shall dare to blame those whose longing to know may be but the yearning of the Spirit of Humanity to rise to some higher plane?

THE THEOSOPHICAL SOCIETY.

Before showing the method suggested in Theosophical teachings for obtaining light on the above questions, or sketching the view of the universe given by Occult Science, it may be well to remove some misconceptions concerning the Theosophical Society, my adhesion to which has brought on my devoted head such voluminous upbraiding. I fear that the objects of the Society will come somewhat as an anti-climax after the denunciations.

They are three in number, and anyone who asks for admittance to the Society must approve the first of these:

1. To be the nucleus of a Universal Brotherhood.

2. To promote the study of Aryan and other Eastern literatures, religions, and sciences.

3. To investigate unexplained laws of nature and the psychical powers latent in man.' Nothing more! Not a word of any form

of belief; no imposition of any special views as to the universe or man; nothing about Mahatmas, cycles, Karma or anything else. Atheist and Theist, Christian and Hindu, Mahommedan and Secularist, all can meet on this one broad platform, and none has the right to look askance at another.

The answer to the inquiry, "Why did you join the Society?" is very simple. There is sore need, it seems to me, in our unbrotherly, anti-social civilization, of this distinct affirmation of a brotherhood as broad as Humanity itself. Granted that it is as yet but a beautiful Ideal, it is well that such an Ideal should be lifted up before the eyes of men. Not only so, but each who affirms that ideal, and tries to conform thereto his own life, does something, however little, to lift mankind towards its realization, to hasten the coming of that Day of Man. Again, the third object is one that much attracts me. The desire for knowledge is wrought deep into the heart of-every earnest student, and for many years the desire to search out the forces that lie latent in and around us has been very present to me. I can see in that desire nothing unworthy of a Freethinker, nothing to be ashamed of as a searcher after truth. "We seek for Truth" is the motto of the National Secular Society, and that motto, to me, has been no lip-phrase.

Beyond this, the membership of the Theosophical Society does not bind its Fellows. They can remain attached to any religious or non-religious views they may have previously held, without challenge or question from any. They may become students of Theosophy if they choose, and develop into Theosophists; but this is above and beyond the mere membership of the Society.

This fact, well known to all members of the Society, shows how unjust was the attack on Mdme. Blavatsky, accusing her of inconsistency because she said there was nothing to prevent Mr. Bradlaugh from joining the Theosophical Society. There is nothing in the objects to prevent anyone from joining who believes, as do all Atheists, I think, in the Brotherhood of Man.

While this pamphlet is passing through the press a curious judicial decision on the status of the Society reaches me from America. A Branch Society at St. Louis applied for a Decree of Incorporation, and in ordinary course the Report, based on sworn testimony, was delivered to the court by its own officer, and on this the decree was issued. The Report found that the Society was not a religious but an educational body; it "has no religious creed, and practices no worship." The Report then proceeded to deal with the Third Object of the Society, and found that among the phenomena investigated were "Spiritualism, mesmerism, clairvoyance, mind-healing, mind-reading, and the like. I took testimony on this question, and found that while a belief in any one of these sorts of manifestations and phenomena is not required, while each member of the Society is at liberty to hold his own opinion, yet such questions form topics of enquiry and discussion, and the members as a mass are probably believers individually in phenomena that are abnormal and in powers that are superhuman as far as science now knows-."

Perhaps those Secularists who have been so eager to credit me with beliefs that I have not dreamed of holding, will accept this deliverance of a court of justice, as they evidently refuse to take my word, as to the conditions of membership in the Theosophical Society. When, for instance, I find Mr. Foote in the Freethinker crediting me with belief in the " transmigration of souls," I can but suppose that he is moved rather by a desire to discredit me than by a desire for truth. Indeed, the headlong jumping at unfavorable conclusions, and the outcry raised against me, have been a most painful awakening from the belief that Freethinkers, as such, would be less bigoted and unjust than the ordinary Christian sectary. The Report proceeds: "The object of this Society, whether attainable or not, is undeniably laudable. Assuming that there are physical and psychical phenomena unexplained, Theosophy seeks to explain them. Assuming that there are human powers yet latent, it seeks to discover them. It may be that absurdities and impostures are in fact incident to the nascent stage of its development.

As to an undertaking like Occultism, which asserts powers commonly thought superhuman and phenomena commonly thought supernatural, it seemed to me that the Court, though not assuming to determine judicially the question of their verity, would, before granting to Occultism a franchise, enquire at least whether it had gained the position of being reputable, or whether its adherents were merely men of narrow intelligence, mean intellect, and omnivorous credulity. I accordingly took testimony on that point, and find that a number of gentlemen in different countries of Europe, and also in this country, eminent in science, are believers in Occultism.

The late President Wayland, of Brown University, writing of abnormal mental operations as shown in clairvoyance, says: 'The subject seems to me well worthy of the most searching and candid examination. It is by no means deserving of ridicule, but demands the attention of the most philosophical enquiry.' Sir William Hamilton, probably the most acute, and undeniably the most learned, of English metaphysicians that ever lived, said at least thirty years ago: 'However astonishing, it is now proved beyond all rational doubt that in certain abnormal states of the nervous organism perceptions are possible through other than the ordinary channels of the senses.' By such testimony Theosophy is at least placed on the footing of respectability. Whether by further labor it can make partial truths complete truths, whether it can eliminate extravagances and purge itself of impurities, if there are any, are probably questions upon which the Court will not feel called upon to pass." On this official Report the Charter of Incorporation was granted, and it may be that some, reading this gravely recorded opinion, will pause ere they join in the ignorant outcry of "superstition" raised against me for joining the Theosophical Society. Every new truth is born into the world amid yells of hatred, but it is not Freethinkers who should swell the outburst, nor' ally themselves with the forces of obscurantism to revile investigation into nature.

THEOSOPHY.

It may, however, be granted that most of those who enter the Theosophical Society do so because they have some sympathy with the teachings of Theosophy, some hope of finding new light thrown on the problems that perplex them. Such members become students of Theosophy, and later many become Theosophists.

The first thing they learn is that every idea of the existence of the supernatural must be surrendered. Whatever forces may be latent in the Universe at large or in man in particular, they are wholly natural. There is no such thing as miracle. Phenomena may be met with that are strange, that seem inexplicable, but they are all within the realm of law, and it is only our ignorance that makes them marvellous. This repudiation of the supernatural lies at the very threshold of Theosophy: the supersensuous, the superhuman, Yes; the supernatural, No.

[I may here make a momentary digression to remark that some students quickly fall back disappointed because they have come to the study of Theosophy with conceptions drawn from theological religions of supernatural powers to be promptly acquired in some indefinite way. We shall see that Theosophy alleges the existence of powers greater than those normally exercised by man, and alleges further that these powers can be developed. But just because there is nothing miraculous or supernatural about them, they cannot be suddenly obtained. A student of mathematics might as well expect to be able to work out a problem in the differential calculus as soon as he can struggle through a simple equation, as a student of

Theosophy expect to exercise occult faculties when he has mastered a few pages of the "Secret Doctrine."

A beginner may come into contact with someone whose ordinary life occasionally shows in a perfectly simple and natural way the possession of abnormal powers; but he must himself keep to his ABC for awhile, and possess his soul in patience.

The next matter impressed on the student is the denial of a personal God, and hence, as Mdme. Blavatsky has pointed out, Agnostics and Atheists more easily assimilate Theosophic teachings than do believers in orthodox creeds. In theology, Theosophy is Pantheistic, "God is all and all is God." "It is that which is dissolved, or the illusionary dual aspect of That, the essence of which is eternally One, that we call eternal matter or substance, formless, sexless, inconceivable, even to our sixth sense, or mind, in which, therefore, we refuse to see that which Monotheists call a personal, anthropomorphic God." ("Secret Doctrine," vol. i, p. 545.)

The essential point is: "What lies at the root of things, 'blind force and matter,' or an existence which manifests itself in 'intelligence,' to use a very inadequate word? Is the universe built up by aggregation of matter acted upon by unconscious forces, finally evolving mind as a function of matter; or is it the unfolding of a Divine Life, functioning in every form of living and non-living thing? Is Life or Nonlife at the core of things? Is 'spirit' the flower of 'matter,' or 'matter' the crystallisation of 'spirit'?"

Theosophy accepts the second of these pairs of alternatives, and this, among other reasons, because Materialism gives no answer to the riddles in psychology of which I gave some samples above, whereas Pantheism does; and the hypothesis which includes most facts under it has the greatest claim for acceptance. On the plane of matter, materialistic Science answers many questions and promises to answer more; on the plane of mind she breaks down, and continually murmurs, "Insoluble, unknowable." On the other hand, assuming intelligence as primal, the developed and dawning faculties of the human mind fall into intelligible order, and can be studied with hope of comprehension.

At any rate, where Materialism confesses itself incapable, no blame can be attached to the student if he seek other method for solving the problem, and if he test the methods offered to him by some who claim to have solved it, and who prove, by actual experiment, that their knowledge of natural laws in the domain of psychology, and outside it, is greater than his own. So far, however, as Theosophy is concerned in its acceptance of the Pantheistic hypothesis, it is not necessary to make any long defence. Pantheism, for which Bruno died and Spinoza argued, need not seek to justify its existence in the intellectual world.

The theory of the Universe which engages the attention of the student of Theosophy comes to him on the authority of certain individuals, as does every other similar theory, religious or scientific. But while all such theories are put forward by individuals, there is this broad difference between the tone of the priest and that of the scientific teacher; one claims to rest on authority outside verification; the other submits its authority to verification. One says: "Believe, or be damned; you must have faith."

The other says: "Things are thus; I have investigated and proved them; many of my demonstrations are incomprehensible to you in your present state of ignorance, and I cannot even make them intelligible to you off-hand; but if you will study as I have studied, you can discover for yourself, and you can personally verify all my statements." The Theosophical theory of the Universe comes into the latter category. The student is not even asked to accept it any faster than he can verify it. On the other hand, if he choose to be satisfied with the credentials of its teachers, pending the growth of his own capacity to investigate, he can accept the theory and guide his own life by it. In the latter case his progress will be more rapid than in the former, but the matter is in his own hands and his freedom is unfettered.

I have spoken of "its teachers," and it will be well to explain the phrase at the outset. These teachers belong to a Brotherhood, composed of men of various nationalities, who have devoted their lives to the study of Occultism and have developed certain faculties which are still latent in ordinary human beings. On such subjects as the constitution of man, they claim to speak with knowledge, as Huxley would speak on man's anatomy, and for the same reason, that they have analysed it. So again as to the existence of various types of living things, unknown to us; they allege that they see and know them, as we see and know the types by which we are surrounded. They say further that they can train other men and women, and show them how to acquire similar powers: they cannot give the powers, but can only help others in developing them, for they are a part of human nature, and must be evolved from within, not bestowed from without.

Now it is obvious that, while the teachings of Theosophy might simply stand before the world on their own feet, to meet with acceptance or rejection on their inherent merits and demerits, as they deal largely with questions of fact, they must depend on the evidence whereby they are supported, and, at the outset, very largely on the competence of the persons who give them to the world. The existence of these teachers, and their possession of powers beyond those exercised by ordinary persons, become then of crucial importance. Were the powers to be taken as miraculous, and were they apart from the subject matter of their teachings, I cannot see that they would be of any value as evidence in support of those teachings; but if they depend on the accuracy of the views enunciated and demonstrate those views, then they become relevant and evidential, as the experiments of a skilled electrician elucidate his views and demonstrate his theories.

We, therefore, are bound to ask, ere going any further: do these teachers exist? do they possess these (at present) exceptional powers? The answers to these questions come from different classes of people with different weight. Those who have seen the Hindus among them in their own country, talked with them, been instructed by them, corresponded with them, have naturally no more doubt of their existence than they have of the existence of other persons whom they have met. Persons who are interested in the matter can see these people, cross-examine them, and form their own conclusions as to the value of their evidence. A large number of people, of whom I am one, believe in the existence of these teachers on second-hand evidence, that is, on the evidence of those who know them personally. And this evidence receives a collateral support when one meets with quiet matter-of-course exercise of abnormal faculties, in every-day life, on the part of one alleged to be trained by these very men. A deception kept up for months with absolute consistency through all the small details of ordinary intercourse, without parade and without concealment, is not a defensible hypothesis. And it becomes ludicrous to anyone who, in familiar intercourse, has noticed the quick, impulsive, open character of the much abused and little known Mdme. Blavatsky, as frank as a child about herself, and speaking of her own experiences, her own blunders, her own adventures, with a naive abandon that carries with it a conviction of her truth. (I am speaking of her, of course, among her friends; in face of strangers she can be silent and secret enough.)

It should be added that personal proof of the existence of these teachers is given sooner or later to earnest students, just as, in studying any science, a student after awhile is able to obtain ocular demonstration of the facts he learns second-hand. On the other hand, those who feel that they have attained all possible knowledge and that nothing exists of which they are not aware, can deny the existence of these teachers and maintain, as stoutly as they please, that they are a dream, a fancy. "The Masters," as the students of Theosophy call them, are not anxious for an introduction, and they are not, like the orthodox God, angry with any who deny their existence. Shocking as it may seem to nineteenth century self-sufficiency, they are indifferent to its declaration that they are non-existent, and are in no wise eager to demonstrate to all and sundry that they live. Let it, however, be clearly understood that these teachers have nothing supernatural about them; they are men who have studied a particular subject and have become "masters" in it—Mahatmas, Great Souls, the Hindus call them—and who, because they know, can do things that ignorant people cannot do.

From these Masters, then, say Theosophists, we derive our teachings, and you will find, if you examine them, that they throw light on the nature of man and guide him along the path to a higher life. Man, according to Theosophy, is a compound being, a spark of the Universal Spirit being prisoned in his body, as a flame in the lamp.

The "higher Triad" in man consists of this spark of the Universal Spirit, its vehicle the human spirit, and the rational principle, the mind or intellectual powers. This is immortal, indestructible, using the lower Quaternary, the body, with its animal life, its passions and appetites, as its dwelling, its organ. Thus we reach the famous sevenfold division, or the "seven principles" in man: Atma, the Universal Spirit; Buddhi, the human spirit; Manas, the rational soul; Kama-rupa, the animal soul, its appetites and passions; Prana, the vitality, the principle of life; Linga-sharira, the vehicle of this life; Rupa, the physical body. Theosophy teaches that the higher Triad and lower Quaternary are not only separable at death, but may be temporarily separated during life, the intellectual part of man leaving the body and its attached principles, and appearing apart from them. This is the much talked of "astral appearance," and its reality can only be decided by evidence, like any other matter of fact. Those who know nothing about it will, of course, deride belief in it as superstition, as people like-minded with them derided in the past each newly discovered power in nature. Here again, after awhile, the student has ocular demonstration, and, when he reaches a certain stage, personal experience; but, if he is dissatisfied with secondhand evidence, no blame will fall on him for suspending his belief until he obtains personal proof.

Clairvoyance and allied phenomena become intelligible on this view of man, the projection of the human intelligence, while the body is in a state of trance, taking its place as one of the temporary separations alluded to. The Ego, thus freed, can exercise its faculties apart from the limitations of the physical senses, and has escaped from the time and space limits which are created by our normal consciousness. It is noteworthy that persons emerging from the mesmeric state have no memory of what has occurred during that state, i. e., no impress has been left on the physical organism by the experiences passed through.

But if the seeing or hearing is by the way of the external senses, this could not be for the cerebral activity would have left its trace on the cerebral material.

If, on the other hand, the experiences have been supersensuous, there can be no reason to look for their record in the sense-centers; and the outcome of the experiment is merely the fact that, under these conditions, the Ego is powerless to impress on the physical frame the memory of its actions. So long, indeed, as the lower nature is more vigorous than the higher, this impotency of the Ego will continue; and it is only as the higher nature developes and takes the upper hand in the alliance, that the physical consciousness will become impressible by it. This stage has been reached by many, and then consciousness becomes unified, and higher and lower work in harmony under the control of the will.

The weakening of the body by disease sometimes brings about, but in an undesirable way, a temporary supremacy of the Higher Self, resulting in that keenness of perception referred to on page 10. To obtain such keenness normally, without injury to health, it would be necessary to refine and purify the physical organization, and this, among other things, may be effected in due course.

On the existence of this separable and indestructible entity, the Ego, hinge the doctrines of Reincarnation and Karma. Reincarnation—ignorantly travestied as transmigration of souls— is the rebirth of the Ego, as above defined, to pass through another human life on earth. During its past incarnation it had acquired certain faculties, set in motion certain causes. The effects of these causes, and of causes set in motion in previous incarnations and not yet exhausted, are its Karma, and determine the conditions into which the Ego is reborn, the conditions being modified, however, by the national Karma, the outcome of the collective life. The faculties acquired in previous incarnations manifest themselves in the new life, and genius, abnormal capacities of any kind, possession of knowledge not acquired during the present existence, and so on, are explained by Theosophy on this theory of reincarnation. Infant prodigies, calculating boys, et hoc genus omne, fall into order in quite natural fashion, instead of remaining as inexplicable phenomena. From the point of view of Theosophy, nothing is lost in the Universe, no force is extinguished. Faculties and capacities painfully acquired during the long course of years do not perish at death.

When, after long sleep, the time for rebirth comes, the Ego does not reenter earth-life as a pauper; he returns with the fruits of his past victories, to make further progress upwards.

The only proof of this doctrine, apart from the explanation it gives of the otherwise inexplicable cases of genius, etc., and its inherent probability—given any intelligent purpose in human existence—must, in the nature of things, lie for us in the future if it exists at all; the Masters allege it on their personal knowledge, having reached the stage at which memory of past incarnations revives; the doctrine comes to us on their authority, and must be accepted or rejected by each as it approves itself to his reason.

Similarly, the working of the law of Karma cannot be demonstrated as can a problem in mathematics. The law of Karma has been defined by Colonel Olcott as the law of ethical causation; Theosophists affirm that the harvest reaped by man is of his own sowing, and that, although not always immediately, yet inevitably, every act must work out its full results. We may argue to this law in the mental and moral worlds, by analogy from the physical. Each force on the physical plane has its own result, and where many forces interact, each has, none the less, its complete effect. On the higher planes, since the Universe is one, we may reasonably look for similar laws, and one of these laws is Karma. That it will be difficult to trace its exact working in any instance lies in the nature of the case. We may see a body rushing in a given direction, and we know that the line along which it is travelling is the resultant of all the forces that have impelled it; but that resultant may have been caused by any one of a thousand combinations, and in default of the knowledge of the whole history of its motion we cannot select one combination and say, such and such are the forces.

How then can we expect to perform such a feat in the more complicated interplay of all the Karmic forces that ultimate in the character and environment of an individual? The general principle can be laid down; for the working out of a particular case in detail we have not the material.

One of my critics, Mr. G. W. Foote, asks me how I can reconcile Karma with Socialism, and he affirms that the Socialist, and "every social reformer, is fighting against Karma." Not so in any effective sense. To bring fresh forces to improve the present is not to deny the effects of past causes, but is only to introduce new causes which shall modify present effects and change the future. It may well be that the present poverty, misery, and disease spring inevitably from past evil, and this all scientific thinkers must admit, whether or not they use the word Karma; but that is no reason why we should not start forces of wisdom and love to change them, and create good Karma for the future instead of continuing to create bad. By every action we modify the present and mould the future; that the past has created so evil an heritage but makes the need the sorer for strenuous effort now. It must be remembered that Karma is not a personal Deity, against whose will it might be thought blasphemous to contend. It is simply a law, like any other law of nature, and we cannot violate it even if we would. But it no more prevents us from aiding our fellow-men than " the law of gravitation " prevents us from walking upstairs. We cannot prevent a man from suffering physical pain if he breaks his leg, but the law of nature that pain follows lesion of sensitive tissues does not hinder us from nursing the sufferer and alleviating the pain as much as possible. Neither can we save a man from the sway of Karmic law, but there is nothing to prevent us from trying to lighten his suffering, and above all from endeavoring to put an end to the causes which are continually generating such evil results. Does Mr. Foote deny that all around us is the outcome of past causes? or does he say that because there is causation we must sit with folded hands in face of evil? The true view, it seems to me, is that as present conditions are the results of past activities, so future conditions will be the results of present activities, and we had better bestir ourselves to the full extent of our powers to set going causes that will work out happier results.[1] What belief in Karma does is to prevent mere idle and useless repining, and to teach a dignified and virile acceptance of inevitable suffering, while bracing the spirit to sustained endeavor to improve the present and thus inevitably improve the future.

Nor must it be forgotten that courage to face pain, and love, and generous self-sacrifice for others, are all of them Karmic

---

[1] *See an article, "Karma and Social Improvement," by the present writer, in Lucifer for August, 1886. The question is there more fully worked out.*

fruits, effects of past causes and themselves causes of future effects. The religionist, who hopes to escape from the consequences of his own misdeeds through some side-door of vicarious atonement, may shrink from the stern enunciation of the law of Karma, but the Secularist who believes in the reign of law can have no quarrel on this head with the Theosophist.

Difference can only arise when the Theosophist says: "' You must pay every farthing of the debt run up, either in this or in some future incarnation." The non-Theosophical Secularist would consider that death cancels all debts. To the Theosophist death merely suspends the payment, and the full undischarged account is presented to the dead man's successor, who is himself in a new dress.

Theosophy further teaches, in connection with man, that he may develop by suitable means not only the psychic qualities of which glimpses are given in the abnormal manifestations before alluded to, but power over matter far greater than he at present possesses, and psychic abilities in comparison with which those now looming before us are but as the capacities of infants to those of grown men. In the slow evolution of the human race these qualities will gradually unfold themselves; further, they may be, so to say, "forced" by any who choose to take the requisite means.

And here comes in the asceticism to which Mr. Foote so vehemently objects; he declares that the acceptance of celibacy by an individual for a definite object implies that "Marriage is now a mere concession to human weakness. Celibacy is the counsel of perfection. The sacred names of husband and wife, father and mother, are to be deposed as usurpers. At the very best they are only to be tolerated. It is idle to reply that celibacy is only for the 'inner circle.' If it be the loftiest rule of life, it should be aimed at by all." With all due respect to Mr. Foote, his denunciation savors somewhat of claptrap, though well calculated to appeal to the ordinary British Philistine of Mr. Matthew Arnold.

No one wants to depose any names, sacred or otherwise, as usurpers. It sounds rather small after this tremendous objurgation, but all the Theosophist says is, if you want to obtain a certain thing you must use certain means; as who should say, if you want to swim across that swift current you must take off your coat.

But if it be good, should not everyone try for it? Not necessarily. Music is very good, but I should be a fool to practice eight hours a day if I had but small talent for it; if I have great talent, and want to become a great artist, I must sacrifice for it many of the ordinary joys of life; but is that to say that every boy and girl must fling aside every duty of life and practice incessantly, without the slightest regard to anything else? Only one out of millions has the capacity for that swift development to which allusion is made, and celibacy is one of the smallest of the sacrifices it demands for its realization. The spiritual genius, like other geniuses, will have its way, but Mr. Foote need not fear that it will become too common, and

Theosophy does not advise celibacy to those not on fire with its flame.

I ought perhaps in passing to say a word as to the power over matter spoken of above, because a good deal of fuss, quite out of proportion to their importance, has been made about the "phenomena" with which Mdme. Blavatsky's name has been associated, and many people assume that it is pretended that they are "miracles," or are a phase of "Spiritualistic manifestations."

The bitter attacks made on Mdme. Blavatsky by Spiritualists ought to convince unprejudiced people that she has not much in common with them. As a matter of fact, her main object in the greater number of cases, as she said at the time, was to show that far more remarkable things than were done among Spiritualists by "spirits" in the dark could be done in full daylight without any "spirits," merely by the utilization of natural forces. All that she claimed was that she knew more about these forces than did the people about her, and could therefore do things which they could not. A good many of the apparent miracles turned merely on the utilization of magnetic force, a force about the marvels of which science is finding out more year after year. Mdme. Blavatsky is able to utilize this force, which everyone admits is around us, in us, and in nonliving things, without the apparatus used at the present time by science for its manipulation. Other of the phenomena were what she called "psychological tricks," illusions, conjuring on the mental plane as does the ordinary conjurer on the material, making people see what you wish them to see instead of what really is. Others, again, were cases of thought-transference.

Another group, that including the disintegration and reintegration of material objects, is more difficult to understand. All I can say myself as to this is that when I find a person, who leads a good and most laborious life, and who exercises powers that I do not possess, telling me that this can be done and has been done within her own knowledge in a perfectly natural way, I am not going to say "deception," "charlatanry," merely because I do not understand; any more than I should say so if Tyndall told me of one of his wonderful experiments, as to which I did not understand the modus operandi.

There remains a great stumbling-block in the minds of many Freethinkers, which is certain to prejudice them against Theosophy, and which offers to opponents a cheap subject for sarcasm—the assertion that there exist other living beings than the men and animals found on our own globe. It may be well for people who at once turn away when such an assertion is made to stop and ask themselves whether they really and seriously believe that throughout this mighty Universe, in which our little planet is but as a tiny speck of sand in the Sahara, this one planet only is inhabited by living things? Is all the Universe dumb save for our voices? eyeless save for our vision? dead save for our life?

Such a preposterous belief was well enough in the days when Christianity regarded our world as the center of the

Universe, the human race as the one for which the creator had deigned to die. But now that we are placed in our proper position, one among countless myriads of worlds, what ground is there for the preposterous conceit which arrogates as ours all sentient existence? Earth, air, water, all are teeming with living things suited to their environment; our globe is overflowing with life. But the moment we pass in thought beyond our atmosphere everything is to be changed. Neither reason nor analogy supports such a supposition. It was one of Bruno's crimes that he dared to teach that other worlds than ours were inhabited, but he was wiser than the monks who burned him. All the Theosophist avers is that each phase of matter has living things suited to it, and that all the Universe is raising with life. " Superstition" shriek the bigoted. It is no more superstition than the belief in Bacteria, or in any other living thing invisible to the ordinary human eye. "Spirit" is a misleading word, for, historically, it connotes immateriality and a supernatural kind of existence, and the Theosophist believes neither in the one nor the other. With him all living things act in and through a material basis, and "matter " and "spirit " are not found dissociated. But he alleges that matter exists in states other than those at present known to science. To deny this is to be about as sensible as was the Hindu prince who denied the existence of ice, because water in his experience never became solid. Refusal to believe until proof is given is a rational position; denial of all outside our own limited experience is absurd.

MINUTIAE.

Before closing this explanatory pamphlet I must allude to the kind of weapons being used against me by one or two writers in the Freethinker. I speak of it here because I have no other way of answering the paragraphs which appear in that journal week after week, and I will take two or three as specimens of a kind of controversy which is not, I venture to think, worthy of the Freethought cause.

"Mrs. Besant goes in for the transmigration of souls," and then follows an absurd statement about the souls of ill-behaving Hindu wives passing into various animals. This assertion is worse than a caricature, it is a misrepresentation; and as I am told that Mr. Wheeler "knows more about Buddhism and Oriental thought generally than Mrs. Besant is ever likely to learn," I cannot suppose that the misrepresentation springs from ignorance. No Theosophist believes in the transmigration of souls, or that the human Ego can enter a lower animal; and a blunder" that might pass from an ignoramus is not excusable where such great professions of learning are made. I take the above statement as a type of the caricatures of Theosophy to be found in the Freethinker.

There are other paragraphs which give a false idea by suppression of part of the truth. Thus: Mr. Foote states that "we do not intend to open our columns for the discussion of Theosophy" (although he had attacked it), and saying that he was going to publish a letter from a Theosophist, he adds: "The Theosophists must not expect to use our columns any further.

Mr. Wheeler reviewed Mdme. Blavatsky's book on its being sent to him for that purpose, and it is not customary to discuss reviews." Putting aside the fact that Mr. Wheeler's article was an attack on Theosophy and on Mdme. Blavatsky personally, rather than a review of the "Secret Doctrine," the above sentence implies that the criticism of the Freethinker was challenged by the Theosophists sending the book. This was not so: Mr.

Wheeler wrote saying that my adhesion to Theosophy would cause interest in the subject to be felt by Freethinkers, and asking for a copy of the book for review. This was an unusual course to take as preface to a bitter personal attack, but, waiving the question of literary courtesy, the point is that the initiative came from the Freethinker, not from the Theosophists. It is not consistent with Freethought traditions to gratuitously attack a person and then decline discussion. Again, Mr. Foote writes: " We do not agree with the Medium and Daybreak that Mr. Foote should have treated Mrs. Besant's 'apostacy with silent contempt.' A very different treatment was called for by her character and past services to the cause." The words in inverted commas do occur in the Medium and Daybreak, but the context considerably alters the meaning suggested by them as quoted by Mr. Foote. The passage runs: "'Mrs. Besant's Theosophy' is the title of a 16-page two-penny worth by G. W. Foote, in which 'the Freethought party' is an ominous-phrase. Like the 'Church' it stands high above truth, and Mrs. Besant is censured for treating it so 'cavalierly.' In view of the lady's new style of propaganda, Mr. Foote is anxious for the 'interests of the Freethought party.' If the 'philosophy' of that body be so 'sound and bracing,' why the weakness of Mrs. Besant, and the dangerous tendencies of her new views? Mr. Foote would have shown laudable consistency, and more no-faith, if he had treated her apostacy with silent contempt."

Comment is needless.

Then we have a number of personal attacks on Madame Blavatsky; has not Mr. Foote suffered enough from the slanderous statements of opponents to hesitate before he gives currency to malignant libels on another? What would he think of me if I soiled these pages with a repetition of the stories told against him by the lecturers of the Christian Evidence Society? Yet he adopts this foul weapon against Madame Blavatsky. "No case; abuse the plaintiff's attorney." How utterly careless Mr. Foote is in picking up any stone that he thinks may inflict some slight injury is shown by the following paragraph: "We learn on the authority of a Theosophist that Madame Blavatsky is going abroad for a few months, and has confided the presidentship of the Theosophical Society into the hands of her new convert, Mrs. Besant." The matter is trivial enough—save for the ungenerous attempt to make out that the Theosophical Society must be hard up for adherents if it had to fall back on a new member as acting president—but it happens that Madame Blavatsky is not the president of the Theosophical Society, and has never held that position. No "Theosophist" could have made such a blunder, but a sneer was wanted, so accuracy was thrown to the winds.

My chief reason for drawing attention to these blunders is to show that I have some cause to ask Freethinkers not to adopt, without examination, Mr. Foote's statements about the beliefs or the lives of Theosophists, but to justify their name by making personal investigation before they decide.

TO MEMBERS OF THE NATIONAL SECULAR SOCIETY.

One last word to my Secularist friends. If you say to me, "Leave our ranks," I will leave them; I force myself on no party, and the moment I feel myself unwelcome I will go. It has cost me pain enough and to spare to admit that the Materialism from which I had hoped all has failed me, and by such admission to bring upon myself the disapproval of some of my nearest friends. But here, as at other times in my life, I dare not purchase peace with a lie. An imperious necessity forces me to speak the truth as I see it, whether the speech please or displease, whether it bring praise or blame. That one loyalty to Truth I must keep stainless, whatever friendships fail me or human ties be broken. She may lead me into the wilderness, yet I must follow her; she may strip me of all love, yet I must pursue her; though she slay me, yet will I trust in her; and I ask no other epitaph on my tomb, but She tried to follow Truth.

THE END.

THE END.

Made in the USA
Las Vegas, NV
27 January 2022

42441312R00056